Thailand
Andaman Sea
Stephen Platt

www.leveretpublishing.com

Thailand: Andaman Sea
First published - January 2018
Published by
Leveret Publishing
56 Covent Garden, Cambridge, CB1 2HR, UK

ISBN 978-1-9124601-5-1

© Stephen Platt 2018

All rights reserved. No part of this publication may be reproduced, stored in a retrieval system or transmitted in any form by any means, electronic, mechanical, photocopying, recording or otherwise, except brief extracts for the purpose of review, without the written permission of the publisher.

Thailand
Andaman Sea

Thailand 2009

Bangkok

Saturday 31 January 2009
Six of us went to Thailand to survey a fishing village called Ban Nam Khem four years after the 2004 Indian Ocean tsunami. The idea was to see if we could use satellite imagery to monitor long-term disaster recovery. It was my birthday and only six months since I had a new hip and I was worried about being cramped, but to my surprise and delight the seats were roomy and I watched a film and fell asleep.

The taxi journey was easy apart the security guards sweeping under the taxi with a mirror looking for a bomb as we got to the Centre Point Hotel. I was on the 22nd floor and my balcony overlooked the American Embassy, an old house in a large garden. The room is spacious, with a large opening between the bathroom and bedroom, which made it feel rather decadent. We had an excellent meal in the hotel restaurant then got together at a round table on the porch outside to plan.

View from my hotel window looking south to American Embassy gardens

Monday 1 February

Bangkok is hot and steamy, like a concrete jungle. Keiko, my Japanese colleague from Cambridge, says all the cities of the Far East are the same – there was a building boom in the 80s and much of the old architecture was swept away and leaving somewhat repellent chaotic development and commercial anarchy. It was hot; Torwong said when he was a child he remembered cold winters when he had to wear a sweater to school, now the temperature never drops below 20°C.

The sky train was full of young people commuting to work and to the University at the end of the line. All six of us crowded into a taxi with me in the front clutching all our bags. Our meeting was in the Department of Fisheries and Coastal Protection, which was hosting a week long fair, to which people bring their produce and livestock from the country for sale at long lines of stalls winding through the campus.

The presentations went well and at coffee time an old man served sticky rice and banana toffee delicacies wrapped in vine leaves. He was there again at lunchtime with three or four delicious meals of chicken, fish, vegetables and

View from my hotel window looking north to Sky-train

sweet-and-sour curry. All this for just a small meeting! Ratana was in a good form chairing the meeting but my heart sank when she said we would work on the survey after the meeting. I was dead on my feet and had nearly drifted off to sleep, but she was right the questionnaire needed a lot of work and we had to do it before she and Dr Kunwan left for Ban Nam Khem. Poor Daniel found it hard listening to her gentle probing and its implied criticism but we got some important feedback, not least that it might help to have two versions – one for key informants and the other for households and that it should be shorter. I decided to work on it tomorrow.

Eventually we were done and we walked across the campus past the fish tanks and ponds to where the market was happening and the long avenue of stalls, shaded by mesh roof strung between the trees and electricity poles. There was a thick press of young people drifting along and stalls selling hot food, plants, puppies and rabbits. We grabbed a cab back to the hotel for a quick rest before venturing out to find a restaurant in the nearest shopping centre. These emporia run along either side of the sky train and are linked by aerial walkways. We found a Thai restaurant and ordered.

Street market near the university

Tuesday 2 February

I woke early and got up to redo the indicator table so it would be easier to use when the team went off to interview Dr Malik at the World Health Organisation. There is a huge assortment of food for breakfast, including all sorts of exotic dishes, but I had got the measure of what I liked. Torwong has curry; he says that breakfast is just another meal. I went back to my room and worked on the survey but was disturbed by the maid wanted to clean the room so I went down to the restaurant and got a coffee and continued to work at a table in the lobby.

I finished about midday and managed to grab a quick catnap before Keiko called to say they were back and we had lunch together in the hotel. We caught a taxi to the old town and went to Wat Pho, perhaps the most famous of the Buddhist temples and the one with a 45m Golden Buddha. The atmosphere was relaxed and no one bothered you about taking photographs. You only had to take off your shoes to enter the temple. The most interesting things were the murals in the open loggias detailing pressure points that were used for teaching Thai massage. Torwong said the Temple had been founded by

Golden Buddha in temple of Wat Pho

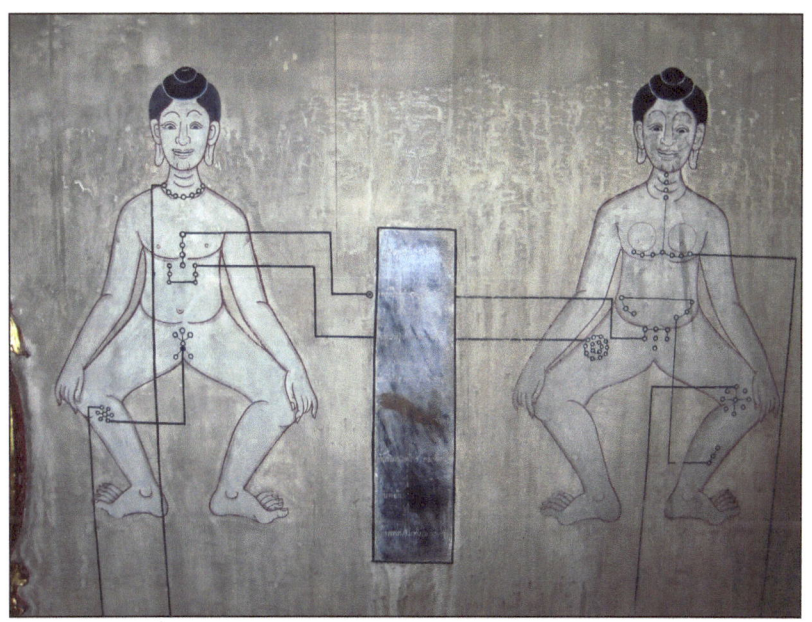

Thai massage murals on walls of temple loggia

We set off on a boat tour of Bangkok waterways

a Thai king who was fond of Chinese art and the huge stone statues had come as ballast in junks. The courtyard outside the temple was shaded by an ancient Bho tree, which gave its name to the name of the temple. There are families with small children on the temple jetty throwing food to the fish.

From there we walked through a market to the water front and a timber pier where we climb aboard a slender skiff with a high pointed prow an outboard motor made from a huge truck engine and a long propeller like one in a James Bond movie. We leave the main river and take a narrow canal. Apparently Bangkok had many more canals but most have been filled in to make roads to ease traffic congestion. Houses crowd to the edge of the canal; some are ramshackled and others are beautifully maintained, some are clearly home-made and others are lavish. Many have verandas and ingenious seating arrangements. They are open to the sky and you can see pots and pans hanging from hooks and clothes drying. People wave. Other boats pass making waves. The water is very shallow; the tide is going out. We see a huge lizard, a relative of the Komodo dragon, basking on the concrete embankment. We stop at a Wat and buy bags of coloured rice to throw to the catfish. It is

The water is shallow and the boats have long propeller shafts from truck sized engines

forbidden to fish near temples so they thrive here. Soon there are hundreds competing for the food. Many have grown huge and they splash water into the boat in their eagerness.

It was getting dusk as we rejoined the main river, passing brightly illuminated hotels and office towers. The Millennium Hilton with its circular roof-top restaurant had fires burning outside like a scene from Apocalypse Now. We were dropped off near the Hotel Oriente, the famous Bangkok Hotel where Conrad stayed. We walked to the sky train along a shopping street and I persuaded John to go into a tailors and see if he could have a suit made. A made-to-measure in Italian light-weight wool would costs £500. John said he'd think about it. I tried the shirt fabric but it seemed too heavy. We caught the sky train to the Siam Shopping Centre and found a restaurant.

I'm terribly tired during the day and then feel awake when I get to bed so I watch a video until late. Having got off about two I woke imagining a phone call. I had finally got off again and my telephone did actually ring. It was Michael asking if I'd replied to his email. I told him that I'd already sent an email and he seemed a bit nonplussed asked if I was stuck anywhere. Maybe he had

Bangkok at night

forgotten I was in Thailand and wondered why I wasn't in work. I said I was fast asleep and that seemed to really throw him. I had difficulty getting off again and was finally in a deep sleep when the phone beeped the message from Scharlie saying she got back safely from Oxford.

In the morning we set off early to visit the Department of Disaster Management and Protection the agency responsible for coordinating all disaster management agencies. We were warned we would hit heavy traffic getting downtown but in the event we had little problem. The Department is a complex of government offices and in the old parliament building we found a place selling coffee and a stone bench and table to sit and wait till nine. A pretty girl came and found us and asked if we were from Cambridge and we were shown into a meeting room. The problems with meetings here is the noise of the air conditioning. It's so loud it's very difficult to understand what people say because they speak quietly. The lady we have come to see is a harassed little woman in her mid-50s huddled with Torwong while Beverly and I try to make conversation with her boss, the Director of the Department and a junior civil engineer. Both have good English but neither knew much about

John presenting our work on imagery analysis

the data that was being collected and the Director wanted to talk about opportunities for study in the UK and about football rather than work. He is a Liverpool fan. I tried on various occasions to unite the meeting but Torwong was locked in deep conversation. Finally we managed to get away and catch a taxi back to the hotel.

I sleep that afternoon and in the evening we walk to the night market that covers a huge area selling the usual mixture of cloths, pirate CDs, phony watches and handicrafts etc. I saunter up the aisles trying to get into the mood to buy presents but find it very off-putting and after an hour or so we meet up and find a restaurant nearby and have a meal. I'm hungry not having eaten since breakfast. I walk back to the hotel while the others take a tuck-tuck.

Night market selling food, clothes and pirated DVDs

Ban Nam Khem

Wednesday 3 February

We planned to leave for Ban Nam Khem at eight but we were slow getting started because we had to make copies of the survey.

It was a long 10-hour drive and I dozed. We had to detour because there was a protest and the police had closed the road and we crossed the mountains to the west coast where the rock is limestone and the vegetation is lush. The hotel is a look-a-like Shangri-La, with a long wooden staircase to the lobby and high ceiling open space.

I had 20 minutes before we'd arranged to meet for dinner, so I had a quick shower and before and walking to the beach and finding a rustic restaurant that cooked us fresh fish to the sound of the waves. After the meal we took off our shoes and strolled in the milky warm waters of the Andaman Sea.

Our hotel in Ban Nam Khem – the Royal Bangsak Resort

Thursday 4 February

I woke just before six after a good sleep and walked down to the sea for a swim. It was just getting light I left my clothes on the high waterline and waded in the water was like warm milk. The sea is cloudy and there is a slight swell. This is the first time I've been swimming since the operation and I felt trepid even though the beach shelved gently and the sea was calm. I stayed in half an hour; I must go more often it feels good for me. I washed the sand off; there is still no one about.

None of my colleagues were up so I chatted over breakfast with one of the group from the University. After typing the results from the indicator survey I grabbed my hat and bag and met the others in the car park. We have a much more productive meeting with the sub district officials than those we had in Bangkok. It confirmed that you learn more by getting closer to the problem in the field.

We were told that there was masses of relief aid, and local services were re-established within 5–6 month, but people are only just beginning to re-establish their independent livelihoods. Many died and many left because

Early in the morning I have the beach to myself

they were afraid of being near the sea there are fewer people than before. One effect has been family division. Large families that previously occupied a single house now have two or three. These families have also grabbed extra boats and outboard motors. Four years on, perhaps because of the huge levels of aid, there are few new businesses and people are only now accepting that they need to rebuild their livelihoods. How well a group did depended a lot on the quality of local community leadership.

We have lunch in a roadside restaurant; a lean to with open sides with homemade plastic screens that roll down like blinds if it rains. We have the same marvellous mix of dishes – mainly fish and prawns with wonderful spicy and aromatic flavours. The problem is that I'm feeling weak. I wonder if there is something wrong with me or if it's just the heat and think about going back to the hotel for a sleep. It's hot in the restaurant but the vegetation crowds in either side and the air is fresh. There are caged birds; this seems popular here. In the event I decide to stick with the team and go off to meet community leaders in the community hall in Ban Nam Khem. The young headman seems very relaxed and tells the story with amusing anecdotes in Thai that we can't

Meeting with community leaders in Ban Nam Khem

understand.

People here look quite different from the people in Bangkok. Three or four of the men sporting toothbrush moustaches look like brothers. This is a Muslim area and the southern region of Thailand was once known as the Pattani Kingdom, an Islamic Malay kingdom established in the 19th century, but later annexed to Thailand. So maybe they came from Malaya originally. The deputy community leader is a small energetic man who gets animated when we get out the big aerial photos and pin them to the wall. This proves very useful, as it seems we have misinterpreted a number of key features.

There are photos pinned up on the walls outside the meeting room and I spot our informants in various shots. There are also a few dozen lifejackets hanging from nails around the room and I'm not quite sure what there are for. Ratana wants to go straight to dinner. Dr Kunwan has invited us and we have persuaded her to let us go via the hotel for a quick wash. As we're leaving the deputy leader tries to organise a football match with it but there is little enthusiasm. The young headman is lighting a spliff as we leave. No wonder he seemed so relaxed, I think. He offers me a toke but I say I've given up smoking.

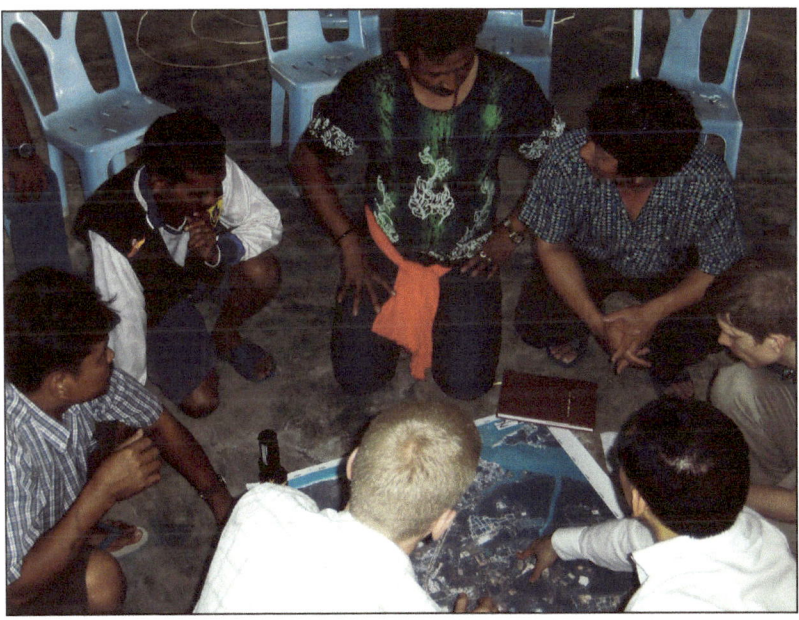

People get excited when we get out the large aerial photographs

The restaurant is on a secluded cliff top above a cove and not that well signed from the road so unlike the roadside bars in Kowlak it has not attracted foreigners. The others have arrived ahead of us and are eating and working on the survey, going through each question and making sure they understand them; it's all very professional.

We have another great meal and when we get back to the hotel Ratana and Dan are hard at work in the hotel lobby. It's cool here in the evening and I go to my room and get my computer and phone Scharlie on Skype. The light from the computer screen makes me look pale and this worries Scharlie and I promise I'll take care and go to a doctor if I get worse.

7 February Saturday
Today we begin the survey. We drive to Ban Nam Khem and stop at a bike repair shop. The owner is the deputy we met yesterday. His shop is a lean-to. It can be closed off with a roll down door and houses his tools and spares. There is an additional lean-to, which he uses as a work area and what looks like a meeting place for the village council.

Working on the survey questionnaire in the cool of night in the hotel lobby

We interview the deputy mayor of the town in his puncture repair shop

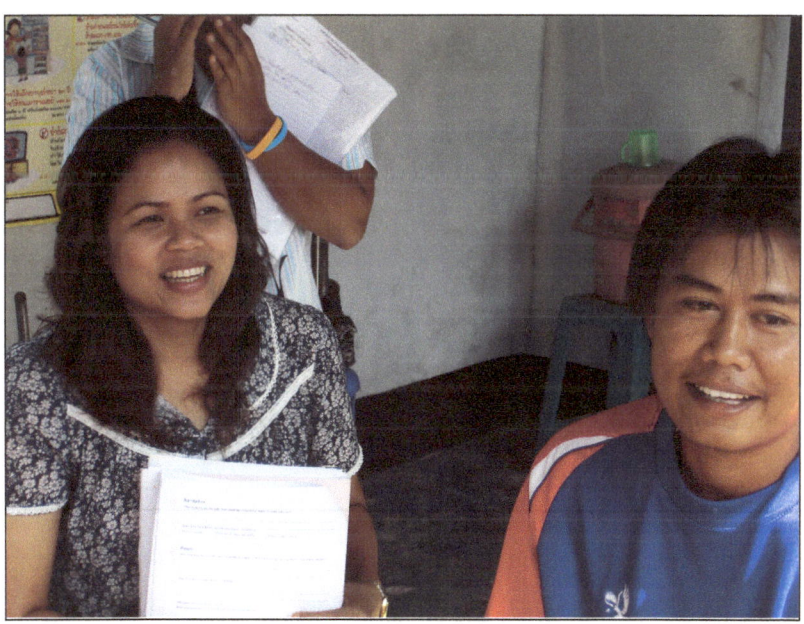
Nat interviews a young fisherman

Nat interviews a young fisherman. He and his brother and father live near the harbour. They were having breakfast when they got a warning and ran for it. They lost everything. The interview seemed to go well. I watched and Ratana made notes and intervened occasionally but Nat seemed very good at interviewing. She smiled a lot and led the interview well.

I was particularly intrigued by a photograph in an album that the bike shop owner let us look through. It showed a mural of a tsunami towering over and engulfing a palm tree and house. The bike shop owner was doing a roaring trade and fixed four rear wheel punctures in 45 minutes while the survey was being done. He was very efficient changing the inner tube and swept up after himself and kept his tools neatly. The shop is in a prime location at a T-junction in the centre of the village. Finally he's done and Ratana starts the key informant interview with him. Dr Kunwan and the other two men suddenly get interested in certain parts of the questionnaire and start to intervene. It's questions about compensation and livelihood that excite the most. The bike shop owner seems to be a good informant from the appreciative noises the other interviewers make.

Child's painting of the tsunami engulfing a house

We finish and go for lunch. The plan for the afternoon is for the girls to continue interviewing on their own while our team do the Views survey. I plan to go back to the hotel for a sleep and see if I can get myself sorted. Ratana and Dr Kunwan have left for a meeting on the coast and won't be back. Ratana says she's looking forward to going back to Canada to the cold weather.

They dropped me at the hotel and after a brief read I go to sleep until four and doze until nearly 5 when I go down to the beach to catch the late sun. The heat is gone and most people are leaving the beach team as I arrive and go for a swim. Keiko has gone into Kowlak to buy a swimsuit and we arranged to meet at 7 in the restaurant on the beach. I get there first; it's only a rude hut with an open kitchen at the back but they produce the most fabulous food. I have steamed fish with lime sauce and lemon juice to drink rather than beer. I decided I need to get fit and I leave at 9 and sleep fairly well until 4.30 and then read until 6 and I get up and go for a swim.

Meals of fresh fish and exotic spices, all made in a rude kitchen on the beach

Sunday 8 February

It is just light and there is no one about this early in the morning. I wrap my room card in my towel and stuff it in the crook of the flagpole. I swim for half an hour and feel stronger than I did yesterday. The sea is calm and the sky cloudy. I swim on my back and watch birds fly. Rather than go back to my room I decide to go for a walk along the beach south towards the pretty promontory I can see in the distance where there is a thatched hut and some tall trees. I'm feeling so much better that I and I decide to jog. My legs feel better than they done for a long time. Nearer the promontory there are more shells and lumps of coral and lots of holes in the sand were crabs have emerged and I catch sight of one scuttling to the sea. It's about the size of my hand and translucent. Maybe they are the soft-shelled crabs that we've been eating. In amongst the shells and pieces of broken coral there are hermit crabs that tentatively pop their legs out of their shells and rock over so they can walk.

I slow to a walk as I near the promontory. Two men are carrying fishing gear to their boat, a long high-prowed skiff like those in Bangkok. They haul

I walk along to the promontory and watch fishermen preparing their nets

themselves out on their anchor rope and then start the motor. After a false start they soon head out towards the three larger boats I can see on the horizon. We have been told that since the tsunami there are two types of fishing – the inshore prawn fishing, using traditional boats like the one I just saw, and bigger boats with gillnets for the mackerel. Some fishermen we've been told prefer the deeper fishing because it's safer in a storm surge.

I have a shower and go for breakfast and sit apart catching up on my journal. We going into Ban Nam Khem to look at look at the vegetation with Sompoth who's an ecologist and to do some more of the Views survey. Views works like Google StreetMap. John sits with a computer on his lap holding a GPS device out of the window of the minibus as we drive along. The GPS records our position as a point on the base image every two seconds. Torwong and Daniel video either side of the van and their cameras are synchronized to the GPS. Later the video is integrated with the points as a series of still images. This way we have a photographic record of the facade of every building that can be examined by clicking a point on the satellite image. This is obviously very useful in interpreting the satellite photograph and to understand the social economic

Traditional small skiffs for inshore fishing

processes underlying the changes we observe from one image to another.

We are doing two types of survey and collecting statistics and data from the local sub district office. The first is with 12 key informants including community leaders, teachers and women's group representatives. The other is a household survey. From the key informant survey we hope to get a general picture of recovery as it affected the whole community. From the household survey we get stories about what happened to individual families. Both are aimed at understanding why things happened when they did, why houses were built in certain places and why families moved when they did. In this way we can begin to understand the processes driving the changes we observe in the imagery and begin to understand better the time sequences involved in recovery, for example when people go back to work and what triggered this independence.

One of the main objectives of the pilot study is to test the questionnaire. We need to be sure we are asking the right questions in the right way. We also need to reduce the household survey down to the minimum we need to do the job. Ratana thinks we need to do 50 households. My instincts tell me we

John tracks our position on GPS

need a larger sample. She is prepared to consider doing 100 if we can reduce the time needed to interview each household to half an hour maximum. The first one took 40 minutes, so this seems feasible. Counter-intuitively the ideal size of the sample is independent of population size and depends on two things – the variance of what you are measuring and the confidence you want to achieve in the results. In fact, no one actually chooses a sample like this. In my experience generally they apply a rule of thumb of about 30 cases for each of the major categories by which they want to analyse the. How to select which households to sample is also a big issue. Ratana wanted to use a quota sample, choosing a 5 to 10 of homes from each of the main housing and not worrying too much about how these were selected, since many houses may be unoccupied or empty on the day. I'm keen on randomly selecting homes from our list of buildings from the satellite imagery. The problem with this approach is that it may mean we have no sample homes in areas that are important to us and it's much more trouble for the interviewers. I suggested we model a variety of sampling frames when we get back and, having pinpointed a house to survey, the interviewers can choose the nearest occupied dwelling.

Daniel and Keiko video either side of the road.

Poor Daniel is finding this stressful. He'd hoped to have thought through these issues when he wrote his first year paper but with all the work preparing the image analysis he didn't have time to plan the survey. The design of the questionnaire obviously depends on what you want the data for. This bears on the structure his thesis since no one else has the time to exhaustively analyse the survey data. The survey data could be used in an ad hoc way to validate the imagery analysis or we might analyse it independently, describing the various aspects of recovery through time. We would then see if the imagery analysis matched. The purpose of the project as described to the EPSRC is to see to what extent aerial imagery can be used to map recovery and to what extent it needs supplementing with ground surveys, both physical and social. Daniel is at that point in his thesis where he wants to keep his options open. All this suggests to me is that we need at least 100 households in our sample, but I'm pushed to explain why exactly. I'm also torn because I favour really short, simple questionnaires and the household survey is the kind of interview schedule I use with a small sample of 50 people maximum.

We visit the sub district chief. He has a large new house on one of the

Recently made shrimp ponds

wharfs. It's an open area with tall coconut palms. He shows us aerial images produced by a research team from the University in Bangkok and invites us into his house to see a model of the master plan that will promote Eco tourism. The plan suggests recreating some aspects of tin mining in the ponds behind the village. We go to look at the mangroves and Sompoth explains how the mangroves regenerate. We're in an area devoted to shrimp farming. There are four huge new ponds. They have used diggers to excavate square holes about 3m deep. These they have lined with black plastic sheeting that they weigh down with sandbags. Women with scarves and wide straw hats push handcarts laden with bags of sand. They pump water in from the nearby creek once it's finished.

We walk along footpaths next to the creek. The mounds of soft earth Sompoth explains are the work of lobsters. The disturbed earth provides a perfect medium for the mangroves to regenerate in the freshwater. The pioneer species are Phoenix and Nypa palm. The dominant mangrove is Rhizophora Sonneraia on the seaward margins. Sompoth also points out a prickly Acanthus plant like holly that he says is used to make tea.

Young mangrove planted to act as a barrier to future storm surge and tsunami

We do some more Views survey around the school. It's big and looks well equipped. A birdsong competition is taking place on the playing field. Rows of caged songbirds sing their hearts out while intense onlookers crane their necks to see whose bird is producing which song. I would have liked to have stopped longer but lunch beckons and John wants to fit in a housing complex built by ITV the Thai television company. The houses are crammed together in tight rows and look unattractive and uncomfortable with corrugated gypsum roofs and utilitarian doors and windows.

We have lunch at a restaurant on the main road. We have to wait here to collect Lin who is who is replacing Mathee as our guide.

We get back to the hotel and I get on the beach about 3.30 and start work on my tan while writing my journal. In some ways Thailand seems familiar having lived in South America. The similarities are not so much in the high-rise architecture of downtown Bangkok, which Keiko says is common throughout Asia, but in the peripheral commercial areas with their garage like shops with roller blind doors and their wares spilling out onto the sidewalks.

As in Latin America, tacky grandiose projects that have gone to seed with a change in the political climate and a similar lover of flags and flamboyant military uniforms. In every government office there is an organisational chart with photographs of employees in white dress uniforms with lots of gold braid. The similarity is even more striking as we drive south. The tropical vegetation is reminiscent of the forest in Ecuador and Guatemala. The new concrete bungalow style is similar, as are the rustic palm-roof shelters and cooking in open-air kitchens at the back. Only the older structures show a distinctive Thai style as do some of the modern hotels, a pastiche of traditional temple decoration with decorative gables and bright colours. Even the people here in the south look vaguely similar to South Americans in their colouring, stature and even their facial character. After all South American Indians originally came from Asia. There are obviously more than enough differences for you to know you are in Asia, but there are these snatches of familiarity so you feel at home.

I dragged the lounger under the Casuarina trees and lie on my stomach. The sun is too bright to read in this position and I drift off to sleep for half an hour and wake at six and head back to my room. Daniel is just arriving. They must have worked late to finish the survey so we can take the day off tomorrow. I try Skyping, somewhat frustratingly, as the connection fails. The Internet card I bought is something of a swizz since the clock runs faster than the actual time connected and you lose 30% of what you paid for. But at least I get through for a short time.

We drive into Khao Lak and Torwong asks us where we want to eat. I suggest we go back to the place Dr Kunwan took us. We get a table overlooking the sea. There is a big moon and the stars are bright. Lin joins us and we discuss what to do on our day off tomorrow. The choice seems to be a coral island or a jungle walk. We decide on the James Bond excursion. I don't know what it involves so it'll be a surprise.

As were driving through Khao Lak Keiko suggests we stop and buy a swimsuit for Lin. The main road is lined with tourist shops, bars and restaurants. I'm not really interested in all the tat and just people watch. There are lots of Scandinavians and some English. I spot Torwong looking at watches and since Jess asked me to buy her a fake Rolex I go over. Most of them look too chunky but I spot a neat one and get Torwong to ask how much it is. It's only £10 so I buy it. Lin buys a pearl necklace and I see a coral bracelet I think might do as a present for Maddie. I'm pleased other overcome my inhibitions and got presents.

We return to the restaurant on the cliff top overlooking the sea

Phuket

Monday 9 February

Today is a holiday and we have decided to take the day off and go sightseeing. We're going to Phang Nga Np which is in the bay above Phuket. It's billed as James Bond Island in the tourist brochures. It's an hour and a half drive through verdant rural landscape where much of the land is given over to rubber trees. Torwong says they are worked in the early morning, but maybe the work is seasonal, as I can see no sign of the coconut cups filling with gum. I ask if the land is owned by absentee landowners but Torwong thinks these are peasant farmers who work the land they live on. I look out for bamboo structures to photograph for Andrea, but timber seems plentiful and only the roof soffits seem to be made with humble bamboo and all the structural

A fast boat takes us to 'James Bond' Island

members seem to be timber. Torwong thinks the bamboo may be used for farm or rural outbuildings. The bamboo we see is lashed together rather than jointed. It is surprising how little Torwong seems to know about his native land.

We arrive and negotiate a boat to take us all for 1,300 bats, as opposed to 2,800 ballots for each of us if we had booked in the hotel. The boat is similar to the one we went on in Bangkok – long, slim and fast, with a big motor and an awning to keep the sun off us. It's pleasant moving through the water. There is relatively little development, maybe because this is a national park. Larger boats pass filled with tourists; this is obviously a popular place. There are mangroves to our left and we are in a big channel heading out into the bay. To our right there are islands with steep limestone cliffs part vegetated, part clean climbable rock. One island is known as dog rock and under an overhang their cave paintings in red ochre. It is not clear how old they are, maybe Bronze Age.

A huge thumb-shaped rock shelters a community of water people living in buildings on stilts. There is a mosque with a golden dome and the buildings have steep rooms descending in steps to the waterfront. There are jetties for boats coming to the various restaurants and I assume we will come back

A huge rock shelters a community of boat people in Koh Panyi village in Phang Nga

here for lunch. Torwong says the community was established by boat people sheltering from monsoon storms and they wouldn't be able to settle now, as the area is a national park. We enter a sheltered channel behind the rock barrier of a string of islands. A launch turns into the cliff face and we follow and enter a cave that links this sheltered channel to the open sea. Gargoyle stalactites hang down from the roof of the cave and people in the other boat shout to create echoes.

We head for James Bond Isle. It's an island with a sandy beach between two high rocks. There are lots of tourists because this was used as a location in the movie. We pull in alongside the other boats and traverse along a rocky path to a bay that crosses from one side of the island to the other. There are lots of stalls and Torwong buys dried squid. It has a strong briny tang of the withal sweet after-taste and leathery texture. I managed to eat half of mine, then throw the rest away and buy an ice cream to get the taste out of my mouth. A deep cleft has formed where a huge slab has slid away from the rock face and been left leaning against the cliff like a playing card. The rock is limestone and the opposing faces of the cleft are almost perfectly smooth and flat. I never

We follow another boat through the cliff barrier to the open sea

The distinctive rock in front of 'James Bond' island, Phang Nga Phuket

There is carving on a huge limestone slab

We return the launch and head back for lunch

Lunch is at the boat people's village we passed earlier

seen limestone cleaved like this. The Crown Princes has left his signature in a concrete plaque.

Finally we climb back on the launch and head back for lunch. A board walkway winds through the village between stalls selling all the usual mixture of jewellery, handicrafts and cloths. The merchants aren't too pressing and it's pleasant. We settle on one of the huge restaurants and order just before a couple of tour boats arrive, but there still served before us as they must be on a pre-ordered package. There are a party of French on the table next to ours. They are the first non-Scandinavian or English tourists we've seen.

I drop off asleep on the drive back to the hotel so don't get to appreciate the different route the driver has taken for our benefit. That night we dine in the hotel in the beach-side restaurant. It's as good as the other places we've been to. I get a phone call from Malachi and tell them I'm in Thailand and he asks if I'm with Mark, who is here at the same time. I hear him relay my conversation to Fran and Scharlie and it seems bizarre that while I'm here next to a warm ocean they are in winter snow and ice.

A couple selling hot food and fruit drinks from a motor-bike and side-car stall

Ban Nam Khem

Tuesday 10 February
Our last day in paradise and we have a meeting with people in the district offices to see about getting data. I don't hold out much hope. It is like Venezuela with lots of conversation and little information. The head of the district we've met before. Nat and Jip are interviewing his secretary. He dives into a drawer in his desk and retrieves a fresh pink shirt which he appears in a few minutes later. I'm not sure what's happening. I think Sompoth and the girls are doing a key informant interview with him. I think part of the problem is that we haven't defined exactly what we want in terms of data. Daniel and John wanted to find out what they had. I didn't expect this would work. Maybe we can go back later and get what we need.

Daniel and I chat about the key question that has been exercising me – why is housing developed or rebuilt where it is. We talk about each of the various examples of new housing financed by the government and other agencies. There are houses on existing plots in the old village, the ITV development of

A good example of new housing

the main road that looks like I'll a little tatty already, the Danish Crown housing, the Rotary Club housing and a more distant development we haven't seen yet. We speculate about what influences the siting and timing of development. Land price and availability are obvious factors. We know the larger parcels of land were government-owned and we know that there were land disputes over plots within the village and some were subdivided. Families who were registered to vote and had title to their land were accommodated before those without title. There are a large number of immigrants Burmese without papers who were living and working in pan Ban Nam Khem. Many children were orphaned inherit title to land but are currently living in an orphanage. So the situation is complex and land title was a significant factor.

Driving around new developments a lot of homes seem unoccupied. The quota was three people to a house so perhaps some families got an extra house, which they plan to rent or sell later. We hear that some people are renting out houses built by aid agencies. We learn that in the Danish Crown settlement new houses cost about £2,200. The Danish Crown provided 70% of the money and the rest of the financing was with a community mortgage. The houses are reasonably attractive but the plots are small and not big

A deep sea fishing boat. Many were carried inland by the tsunami and remain abandoned

enough to plant a garden or a shade tree, typical of the houses in the main village that have more space around them. Consequently the settlement felt very hot and dusty since the road is still unpaved. Some people obviously take more pride in their homes and have painted the brickwork and planted up pots. Maybe this part government grant, part community mortgage, is a good model for financing new housing. Certainly £12 a month mortgage payments seems within most people's reach.

We visit the tsunami memorial on the headland to the west of the village. There is a garden with a museum building housing photograph montage of the disaster and photos of visiting dignitaries, including Bush the Elder, Clinton and Condoleezza Rice. The monument is impressive, comprising a 200m path bounded on one side by a 2-3m high concrete wall and on the other by leaning tile wall containing plaques to the victims. There is a plaque saying it was to natives by the Thyssen family and at least half the plaques are German. Perhaps this used to be a favourite resort for German tourists. Maybe they

The tsunami memorial in Ban Nam Khem. At least half the names are German

boycott the area now since we haven't heard German spoken since we've been here.

We decide to cross over to the island about half a mile away. There is a five-star hotel that was damaged and we plan to have lunch here. Our longboat is slightly broader in the beam and has a flat bow without the usual high-profile that allows them to board the mopeds and motorbikes that everyone drives around here. We pass a number of larger fishing boats. They are wide in the beam and short in length, with a multi-storey superstructure in the aft half of the ship. These must be for the deep-sea fishing we've heard about. In the museum there were photographs of this type of boat washed up far inland.

A golf buggy meets us and ferries us to the hotel. It is rather splendid in the traditional royal style of central Thailand. Torwong approves of the proportions and says they are classically correct. The huge dining room is virtually empty. A long series of landscaped pools stretched to the sea seemingly merging with the waves. The manager tells us the tsunami struck six days before the gala

We are taken to a hotel for lunch in a golf buggy

39

inauguration of the new hotel. Luckily the main structure wasn't damaged. The main lobby is open, so having smashed through the windows there was little to impede the force of the wave. Even the beautiful hardwood floor with its 60cm wide boards wasn't too badly damaged and only needed re-sanding. They were insured but it still took a year to reopen.

We decamp to the lobby and move two heavy tables together and talk about what we've learnt in the pilot study. The girls from reception bring over glasses of ice water for us and the staff are friendly and helpful. I order green coconut milk which is delicious. Last night John Keiko and Dan stayed up late testing different ways of sampling. They downloaded an add-on for ARCGIS the software we're using to analyse the imagery, which allows us to choose random samples. Back in the UK John had identified every distinct structure and given it a unique reference number. They tried two sampling methods, a simple random sample and a proportional sample. I'd always favoured the simple random sample retirement. Ratana and Torwong had favoured the quota sample. In the event it was clear that the simple random sample approach gave us a better wider spread.

I manage to find an example of bamboo used a structural building material

Back on the mainland I manage to get a photograph of some bamboo structural details for Andrea. Torwong says they aren't authentic and that we will look out for something more ancient on the way back tomorrow. Most of the simple thatched huts are made of timber, not bamboo. I change quickly and get back to the beach for a last couple of hours of sun. I have to write a couple of new questions for the household survey about people's perception of the rate of recovery. I produce two versions that I will try on the others tonight. It gets cooler and I decide to stretch my legs and walk along the beach to where three fishermen are setting nets. It's all very primitive. They have 30m of net suspended from foam balls that they drag out into the shallow water and leave for a few hours. They are very dark from working in the sun. There are some shrimp hatcheries behind the margin of casuarina trees and a house under construction.

We sit on in the fading light; this is our last night and we're reluctant to leave the beach. They are setting up tables for dinner and there is going to be an entertainment. We decide to eat here rather than in the rustic restaurant on the beach. Keiko is reluctant to stay because the entertainment has performing

Our last night and a meal on the beach in front of our hotel

monkeys. We go to change and come back 15 minutes later and nearly every table is taken. I had a word with the maitre d' and he said he would fix a table for us on the sand. There was a huge buffet with more than enough food for everyone. A Thai couple sang old Abba hits in a slightly out of key style. When the monkeys came on Dan and I went to our rooms to get stuff to work on later and we decamped to the lobby.

Wednesday 11 February

I wake at five after a somewhat restless night and get up and grab my towel and walk down to the sea. It is still dark and there is a full moon casting a ribbon of silver from the horizon to our beach. I walk out into the soft caressing sea and swim gently for 10 to 15 minutes before going in for a shower and shave. I finish packing and do a final check and find two pairs of socks hidden in a drawer. Each night the maid turns down the bed and leaves a tropical flower. I've arranged them on the spare bed; there are seven, one for each night we've been here. I put money under the last one and slip out quietly. Surprisingly there are already a couple of families at breakfast.

Daniel and John fix a point they can use to register the satellite images

We set off and say goodbye to Dan in Ban Nam Khem. He's staying a couple more days to look around on his own. He looks a little lost in his straw hat as he waves goodbye. He is having to absorb a lot of information all at once and is pushed and pulled in different directions. Torwong has inherited the Cambridge attitude to students in the way he supervises. He says the problem requires a simple mathematical model. This may be too simplistic an approach for Daniel and Torwong says it may be too difficult for him to supervise Daniel since it is like talking to a brick wall. I say Daniel takes everything on board and he's reflective and likes to think things through. He's dealing with a lot of complexity in a system that doesn't necessarily follow simple rules. This is why he's staying behind I think, in the hope of clearing his mind and sorting out the conflicting advice he's been getting. If he can determine his own focus he should have a good thesis. Then again he may go under in the face of Torwong's dismissive clarity of mind. It comes down to different ways of seeing the world. Dan is interested in understanding complex social processes while Torwong wants him to limit his understanding to gathering data for a model of change that validates the physical recovery we can see in the satellite photographs. He just wants to write a book and I'm not interested in that, says Torwong.

A child pictures the impact of the tsunami

I doze the first part of the journey and wake with a violent stomach cramp and desperately need to go to the toilet. We stop to buy fruit and there are some bamboo shelters, distract myself taking photos of the structural detail. We climb back in the van and everyone except me munches pineapple and mango. I groan when we sail past the service station. Finally we stop and I run in. It's not a pretty sight. I suspect it might be the niçoise salad I had at the hotel on the island. The others laugh and say I should have stuck to Thai food.

We drive on and it strikes me that Europe may be exceptional in controlling urban sprawl alongside its main roads. Once out of the mountains and on the plain there is an almost continual ribbon development alongside the two-lane

Last coconut milk

expressway. What is so incongruous is ugly commercial and industrial buildings next colourful Buddhist temples and paddy fields. It's as though the modern world has overwhelmed and engulfed this golden land without people realising it or being powerless to prevent it. Everywhere there are giant photos of the King and Queen. I think to say that they are brand like the products we see advertised but refrain knowing Torwong is sensitive about the Royal family. He's very conservative and thinks Brown and Labour are too left-wing.

There are also huge photos of monks and someone asked about the Dalai Lama. Torwong says Tibetan Buddhism is different – not an everyday matters but in high-level issues. The Dalai Lama he says interferes in politics and that and that's not the role of the contemplative life of a monk and they should stay in their monasteries and meditate. After awhile I say I think the Dalai Lama has been remarkably restrained in speaking out against the Chinese invasion. I wonder what might happen here if something similar happened. Torwong says that it did when Japan invaded during World War. II He says the issue is different in Tibet because the Dalai Lama is also effectively the head of state.

Yesterday over lunch on the island Torwong had described a little of Buddhist belief and how it had emerged out of Hinduism. Buddha had lived 2500 years ago. Last Monday was the anniversary of his death. Both religions Torwong suggested were primarily concerned with individual well being rather prescribing our relations with the Supreme Being like Judaism or Christianity. Buddhist teaching is about freeing oneself from the wheel of life, from human suffering, and reaching a state of Nirvana when we cease to be mortal and become pure energy. Someone asks if it's wrong to kill a mosquito. There are one or two buzzing around our legs. Torwong says it's bad karma and that we should respect all life. He says some people believe that if a fisherman damages a fish with his hook he will be born again with hair lip. I ask if all disabled are being punished for something they did in a previous life. He laughs and uses the phrase 'it serves them right'. This must be the darker side of Buddhism. I obviously haven't got it. I'm realising that the things I thought were so similar can be dramatically different and I'm seeing this return journey quite differently to the way out. Sights seen from the van that seemed so familiar a week ago now seem exotic and alien. Yet I know you get a distorted view from a speeding vehicle and a short stay in a country.

It turns out that Dr Kunwan booked us into the hotel we stayed at because previously in a hotel in Ban Nam Khem village he had been woken by ghosts.

Someone kept him awake all night, he said, running in the room above. In the morning the staff told him in no one was in that room. He believed the sound was of victims running from the tsunami. Torwong also believes in ghosts. To put it more scientifically he thinks that we are linked in what we can perceive as our universe and that there are other dimensions that are inhabited by spirits of the dead. As we approach Bangkok Keiko asks Torwong if he wants to visit his parents. He says he doesn't know where they live and anyway we don't have time. Why should I inflict myself on them, he asks. I see them once a year in summer. Keiko is astonished. We drop Lin off at her university where she has to give a paper. She is late for her seminar and we hope she's in time. The rush-hour traffic is heavy but we finally make it to the hotel. I grab a shower and do my emailing before going down for dinner..

Thursday 12 February
I wake at 6.30 and shower and pack. At breakfast I explain my plan to do a further test on the sampling. The textbook way of selecting a sample size is based on the variance in the phenomenon and the confidence level one wants to achieve. In practice, however, no one does it this way. For a start, we can't calculate the variance, the dispersion around the mean, until we collect the data. People use instinct and experience and get it wrong either choosing to smaller sample to achieve the confidence level they require or selecting a larger sample than they need and wasting resources. Ratana's instinct is to choose a sample of 50 households in five of the 10 areas of the village. My instinct is to select a random sample of 100 houses.

I suggest we test the suggestions by running the software and seeing what geographic dispersion we get with samples of 30, 50 and 100 households. Torwong thinks this is good idea and John agrees to do it for our next meeting. I'm not sure if Torwong takes the surveys that seriously anyway. I expect he operates best with fairly sparse data and then uses his imagination to develop a predictive model. He gets a kick out of predicting reality and seeing if the data matches. He says it's like a magic privilege view into the secrets of the universe. I can empathise with this even if I have never experienced this kind of pleasure. My own view of the world seems much messier and any insights I get about how society works seem at best provisional. Occasionally I come to some simple understanding and theorise some causal relationship about a regular pattern and then find exceptions and have to revise or abandon the theory. It's half-baked yet this is what makes the world go round.

I say goodbye to John and climb into a taxi to the airport there are only three of us, Keiko, Torwong and me, so we fit in one car easily. The driver follows a stream of vehicles alongside side roads that provide a rat run to the expressway. We have a clear run and get there no time. Passport control is painless we split up and I wander around buying biscuits and dried mango to take back as presents. Everything is much more expensive here than in town. But I have Thai baht to burn. I have a rest and an iced cappuccino in Cafe Nero and the rest does me good. I take some aspirin; I have a headache, am feeling queasy and it's supposed to prevent thrombosis. We've arrived horrendously early and Keiko has gone for a massage. Maybe I'll have one too. I find the massage place and ask for a shoulder massage lasting half an hour. It's fantastically painful and deeply satisfying and costs 450 baht, less than £10. I tip the girl my last hundred; she is young and has a pretty face. There's a Boots opposite and I use my last notes on some paracetamol and saunter down to the gate. This seems much more relaxing than most airports had been to.

We say goodbye to John and catch a taxi to the airport

Keiko and Torwong find me and we board. Keiko has booked me into a bulkhead seat. The only catch is that I'm next to the galley and I have a lady with a tiny baby sitting next to me. The baby is angelically asleep. Only another 12 hours plus journey from Heathrow. I'm reading Coetzee's Diary of a Bad Year, a collection of essays on the state of the world.

It was apparent as we got off the aircraft that the poor woman was struggling with her luggage and baby so I hung back at passport control and helped her by taking one side of the car seat carrier. The baby was wide awake and taking it all in. When we got to the escalator and moving walkways I had to take the weight. We said goodbye at the baggage hall and I left her with a trolley I fetch her.

Finally we had all our bags and went to find a taxi. A gust of cold air hit me as we walked through a gusting snowstorm. The driver wanted £220 to go to Cambridge so we decided to go to King's Cross. He dropped the price to £180 so we stayed with him. The M11 was difficult with cars skidding if they braked hard but we got back safely and I was dropped off at Covent Garden to Scharlie's welcoming arms.

Sunset over the Andaman Sea

www.ingramcontent.com/pod-product-compliance
Lightning Source LLC
Chambersburg PA
CBHW040056100426
42734CB00034B/20